James P. O'Brien '48

June 2015

THE
NINTH AIR FORCE
IN COLOUR

THE NINTH AIR FORCE IN COLOUR

UK and the Continent — World War Two

Roger A. Freeman

ARMS AND
ARMOUR

Arms & Armour Press
An imprint of the Cassell Group
Wellington House, 125 Strand, London WC2R 0BB

Distributed in the USA by Sterling Publishing Co. Inc., 387 Park Avenue
South, New York, NY 10016-8810

Distributed in Australia by Capricorn Link (Australia) Pty Ltd, 2/13
Carrington Road, Castle Hill, New South Wales 2154

British Library Cataloguing-in-Publication data:
A catalogue record for this book is available from the British Library.

ISBN 1 85409 272 3

Edited and designed by Roger Chesneau/DAG Publications Ltd

Cartography by Roger Chesneau

Printed in Hong Kong by Dah Hua Printing Press Co.

Frontispiece:
Captain Edwin O. Fisher was the top-scoring air ace of the 362nd FG with
seven victories, which included four FW 190s shot down on 5 July. His
'scoreboard' includes three V-1 flying bombs and the destruction by
strafing of 25 enemy vehicles and five locomotives. The sortie categories
are fighter-bombing, dive bombing and fighter sweeps. The photograph
was taken at Lignerolles airstrip in late July 1944. (Brian Haynes)

CONTENTS

INTRODUCTION

The offensive Allied air forces of the Second World War came to be classified as strategic or tactical. Broadly, a strategic arm was that with a mission to attack an enemy's war effort beyond his front-line forces, predominantly production and supply facilities, whereas a tactical arm supported ground campaigns, usually with objectives selected through co-operation with the armies.

The United States Army Air Forces' first offensive command, designated the 8th Air Force, with a mission to support an invasion of continental Europe from the British Isles, lost its original tactical units to the 12th Air Force which was formed in the United Kingdom in the autumn of 1942. The 12th Air Force was created to provide air support for the invasion of North Africa later that year, the cross-Channel venture being postponed. The 8th Air Force then had, primarily, a strategic mission using heavy bombers, although it retained a ground support command that could expand to function as a tactical air force for the invasion of Europe scheduled for the spring of 1944. The command would embrace day and night fighter, fighter-bomber, reconnaissance, light and medium bomber, troop carrier and transport flying units, as well as a substantial service and supply element. As this tactical command would follow the armies to the Continent, it was decided that it could no longer function as part of the 8th Air Force but should be given a separate Air Force headquarters.

In a general revision of USAAF commands during the autumn of 1943, the 9th Air Force, the small USAAF contingent that had aided the British advance west along the North African coast from Egypt, had its units turned over to the 12th Air Force and the headquarters, its Commanding General and some of the staff were transferred to the United Kingdom to assume responsibility for the tactical force. Thus, in October 1943, VIII Air Support Command with its flying units and service organizations became the nucleus of the new 9th Air Force. The headquarters was basically a redesignation and upgrading of VIII Air Support Command as, with but a few exceptions, the same staff remained.

The inherited flying units that then served under the 9th Air Force banner were four operational medium bomber groups equipped with B-26 Marauders, a tactical reconnaissance group with an assortment of types, chiefly A-20 Havocs and Spitfires, and two troop carrier groups with the useful Douglas C-47 and C-53. During the winter of 1943–44 the 9th Air Force expanded at an extraordinary rate, so that by the end of May, when the last combat group became operational, its complement ran to 45 flying groups operating some 5,000 aircraft. With the necessary ground units, the total number of personnel involved—more than 200,000—was then greater than that of its progenitor the 8th Air Force.

The Force's bases were widely spread. While the eleven bomber groups were all based in the county of Essex, the fourteen troop carrier groups, although originally intended for five airfield clutches in the Grantham–Newark area, were in the event split between that region and south-west England. This was because the north-eastern locations were too far away from the proposed invasion territory for assault gliders to be towed without risking fuel exhaustion for their tugs. Apart from six bases in the Ashford district in Kent, the tactical fighters and reconnaissance groups were chiefly in the New Forest/Wiltshire areas. The fighter groups and their administering fighter wings were formed into two tactical air commands assigned to support specific US armies; a third was formed when additional armies were brought into action on the Continent.

To meet the changing requirements on the ground, there was much transferring of fighter groups from one tactical air command to another. After the Allies landed on the Mediterranean coast of France in September 1944, two fighter groups were transferred to the provisional United States/French 1st Tactical Air Force supporting the invasion force's drive north. There were other depredations of the 9th Air Force's complement, most notably the transfer of IX Troop Carrier Command with its fourteen C-47 groups to the 1st Allied Airborne Army in September 1944. However, this, like the 1st Tactical Air Force, was a provisional formation and administratively the transferred groups were still considered part of the 9th Air Force.

During the period from 16 June 1944—ten days after the Normandy invasion, when the first P-47 Thunderbolts moved to a beach-head landing strip—to early August all eighteen 9th Air Force fighter groups were transferred to bases in France. By the second week of October 1944 all reconnaissance and bomber groups had followed and the first of three troop carrier wings was moving over. Another troop carrier wing was transferred in the first weeks of 1945 but the last wing, based in the Grantham area, did not move to France until the early spring and one group, the 316th, never did leave England for the Continent.

The fighter groups made numerous moves in France to keep within range of the battle front, many staging through the Low Countries and eventually into western Germany before the end of hostilities. The bombers had their final combat bases in Belgium and northern France. After the end of hostilities some units moved back into France; others remained in Germany on occupational duties, the 9th Air Force assuming this role for the United States contingent.

The 9th was an itinerant force, frequently on the move (particularly the fighter and reconnaissance elements), and personnel tended to have little time to wield cameras. There was also difficulty in obtaining film, particularly Kodachrome colour to fit the standard personal cameras of the time. Kodachrome was the first truly commercial colour process within the reach of every man's pocket and was of extremely high quality. Fifty-year-old transparencies still exhibit remarkably true colours. In fact, in the early days of

Kodachrome, it was the limitations of the cameras that most affected the quality of the work. Compared to the 8th Air Force, with its static bases remaining in Britain, the colour photographic cover of the 9th is far more restricted, particularly where aircraft are concerned. This may be in part due to the fact that, until the closing months of hostilities, few 9th Air Force units flouted the bright colours in the fashion seen on 8th Air Force aircraft.

In the 9th Air Force only bombers had command-authorized group identification colours, following a system using white, yellow and black devices. There were no command-required group markings for fighters or reconnaissance aircraft, and units were left to develop their own schemes. The pattern that emerged involved a different, brightly coloured aircraft nose for each squadron within a group and a portion of the vertical tail surfaces coloured for group identification. However, there were a few groups that had no colour identification markings, while troop carrier groups had no group markings of any kind. The 9th was part of the Allied Expeditionary Air Forces and the use of unit code letters allotted by the British Air Ministry was mandatory, the two night fighter squadrons apparently being the only exceptions to this in the combat role.

The following collection of colour photographs featuring 9th Air Force subjects of the Second World War is arranged by combat group, and a base movements map is provided for each as a guide to its dispositions. Most of the photographs have been reproduced from 35mm transparencies, but in order to cover some units it has been necessary to enlarge frames from 8mm and 16mm colour film. This accounts for the poor quality of some of the illustrations. Moreover, because of the scarcity of colour for some units, rare 35mm shots of poor resolution or focus have been used.

It should be appreciated that in the early 1940s colour photography was still in its infancy: commercial stock was then in the form of transparencies, and colour prints were not generally available until twenty years later. For this book, even after an exhaustive search, colour photographs could not be found for a few units. It is known that many more photographs were taken than are presented here, but it has not been possible to trace them and it may be

Above: *The Joker*, of the 397th BG, prepares for take-off from A-72 Péronne, January 1945. The aircraft is well decorated, with a red cheat line down the centre of the fuselage as well as a red 'eyebrows' and 'chin' emphasis on both engine cowlings. The port engine is named *Grunt* and the starboard unit is identified as *Groan*. The aircraft was an original combat B-26B of the 596th BS, and its comparatively low total of missions—some 40—is explained by its absence from combat for several weeks following an emergency landing at a P-47 base in Normandy. (Stan Walsh)

that they have been destroyed. Even so, the images shown should bring to life something of the visual impact made by the 9th Air Force of the Second World War.

ACKNOWLEDGEMENTS

This presentation of colour photographs has been made possible only through the generosity of many people on both sides of the Atlantic. The collection is the result of a prodigious amount of correspondence over four years in an effort to locate those who had engaged in colour photography or possessed colour transparencies. Veterans' permission to use their work or holdings was given by Tamadge Ambrose, Joseph Antrim, Robert Astrella, Glen Boone, Robert Bowen, William Brinson, Jack Curtis, Richard Denison, Link Derick, Gilbert Estelle, William Furniss, Jack Havener, Mrs Clarence Hayden, Arthur Houston, George Kammermeyer, Ira LaTour, Martin Lippoff, Charles Luenneman, Charles Mann, Frank Mancuso, John Moench, John H. Meyer, Richard Perley, John Quincy, Philip Savides, Zell Smith, Alvaro Sousa, George Spradling, George Vasamuper, Stanley Walsh, Jack Woolner, Stanley Wyglendowski and Skip Young.

Jeffrey Ethell gave access to his extensive collection, Steve Sheflin did expert work enlarging motion picture frames and Trevor Allen and Dave Benfield were particularly helpful in a number of ways. Others who supplied material and information are Albert Allen, Philip Bacon, James Bingman, Hasell Barton, George Cassell, Lewis Cellitti, Mark Copeland, Alan Crouch-man, Stewart Dean, W.B. Elliott, Pat Everson, Walt Fink, Fred Giddings, Don Haffeman, Bill Hess, James B. Hill, Graham Hukins, Tom Ivie, Charles R. Johnson, Brian Jones, Mozart Kaufman, John Nicholls, Ian McKenzie, Robert Mynn, Donald Orcutt, George Pennick, William Pierson, John Rutherford, Sam Sox Jr, Neil Stevens, James Tobin, Alex Vanags-Baginskis, Lloyd Wenzel, Dolphus Whitten Jr, Melvyn Wicks and William Yates.

The compiler also wishes to record his appreciation of those friends and colleagues aiding the production —the redoubtable Pat Keen for her trouble-shooting, Ian Mactaggart for his photographic studio work and Bruce Robertson for his editorial guidance. Jean Freeman and Alison Apricot produced the copy (the faithful Alice having taken another appointment).

To all these and any other persons whose assistance has been inadvertently overlooked, I offer my very sincere thanks.

Roger A. Freeman

10th
PHOTOGRAPHIC GROUP (RECONNAISSANCE)

12th and 15th Tactical Reconnaissance Squadrons; 31st, 34th and 155th Photographic Reconnaissance Squadrons

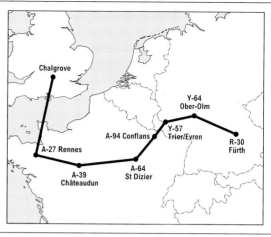

Left: An F-6C of the 15th TRS at St Dizier exhibiting two types of mission symbol—cameras for photographic sorties and binoculars for visual reconnaissance. The aircraft is fitted with a Malcolm cockpit canopy, the bubble shape giving a pilot much better visibility than the original factory type. Tactical reconnaissance squadrons with Mustangs had priority over fighter units for this British-made canopy. The officer posing for the photographer is Captain John Florence. (Ralph Woolner)

Right: Inflatable decoy Mustang look-alikes were often placed on airfields in order to confuse enemy air intelligence as to the disposition of forces. This sorry looking example at St Dizier appears to have sprung a leak. (Ralph Woolner)

Above: Lieutenant-Colonel Robert T. Simpson on an F-6C Mustang of the 15th TRS at St Dizier, autumn 1944. This aircraft was the 'regular ship' of Captain John H. Hoefker, who used it to shoot down three enemy aircraft in June 1944. He became the 10th Group's most successful combatant with credits of 8½ air victories. (Ralph Woolner)

Above: The Stinson L-5 Sentinel equipped some liaison squadrons in the 9th Air Force and a few of these aircraft were also made available to combat groups for communication purposes. This example, photographed at Fürth, is adorned with the dark blue and white checks adopted by the 10th PRG as its identification marking in March 1945. Sergeant Link Derick stands by the L-5's nose. (Link Derick)

Right, upper: Stanley H. Newman's *Azel* of the 162nd TRS at Fürth, Germany, May 1945. Newman was credited with two of the last Luftwaffe aircraft shot down during the war in an action over Czechoslovakia early on VE Day, 8 May 1945. (Stanley Newman)

Right, lower: Another view of Newman's Mustang, showing the camera port in the rear fuselage for oblique photography. The 162nd TRS started out in the 9th Air Force as the 382nd Fighter Squadron, but with the need for more tactical reconnaissance units it was redesignated the 162nd TRS in August 1944. Soon after this it was detached from its original group, the 363rd FG, to serve the requirements of the US armies advancing north from the Mediterranean. The squadron was not assigned to the 10th PRG until the last month of hostilities. (Stanley Newman)

Above: Climbing away from St Dizier, F-5E *Sexy Sal* of the 31st PRS sets out on a photographic reconnaissance mission. This aircraft went missing in action on 29 December 1944. (Ralph Woolner)

Above right: An F-3A, believed to be 43-21731, of the 155th NPS climbs away from Chalgrove. The type was simply an A-20J Havoc fitted out with cameras and flare-dispensing equipment for night photography. Aircraft of the 155th NPS were eventually painted black overall. (Ralph Woolner)

Above: Ralph 'Jack' Woolner and his unusual pet outside a Chalgrove Nissen hut. Fledgeling rooks, taken from the nest, could be reared to become quite tame. (Ralph Woolner)

Left: Returning from a mission, Mustangs of the 12th TRS 'peel off' for landing at their base in Germany. (Ralph Woolner)

31st
TRANSPORT GROUP

87th, 313th and 314th Transport Squadrons; 310th and 325th Ferrying Squadrons

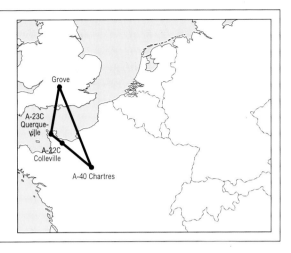

Below: The USAAF's Air Service Command formed its own flying units to handle the transport of cargo and personnel. IX AFASC activated the 31st TG in October 1943 for its requirements but, following the cross-Channel invasion, the group was impressed for air ambulance and general theatre transport work. This Douglas C-53, 42-6484, photographed at Mount Farm, England, in the summer of 1944 with most of its camouflage paint removed, was for long the personal transport of General H. J. F. Miller, who commanded IX AFSC. Its small white triangle shows the identification symbol of the 31st TG. The aircraft arrived in the United Kingdom in February 1943, returned to the USA in August 1945 and was still flying in civilian service in the 1980s. (Robert Astrella)

36th
FIGHTER GROUP

22nd, 23rd and 53rd Fighter Squadrons

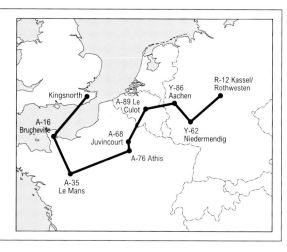

Left to right: 22nd, 23rd and 53rd Fighter Squadron insignia.

48th
FIGHTER GROUP

492nd, 493rd and 494th Fighter Squadrons

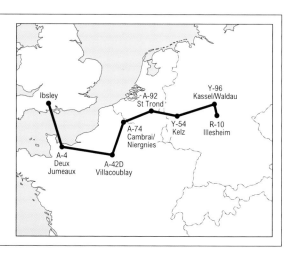

Left to right: 48th Fighter Group shield; and 493rd and 494th Fighter Squadron insignia.

50th
FIGHTER GROUP

10th, 81st and 313th Fighter Squadrons

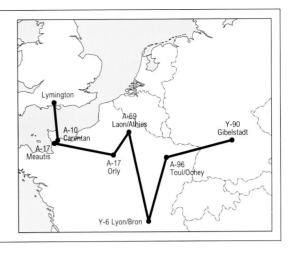

Left: Pilots Lieutenants Philip M. Savides and Richard Perley do a little map studying in a Normandy apple orchard, June 1944. (Richard Perley)

Below: A 50th FG P-47 Thunderbolt lands on the PSP (pierced steel planking) runway cleared of snow at Toul/Ochey, south-west of Nancy, France, in December 1944. A red nose was the Mediterranean Theatre of Operations recognition marking carried by most aircraft of the 1st Tactical Air Force, to which the 50th FG was assigned during the last seven months of hostilities. (Philip Savides)

Above left: Latrine humour: Lieutenant Richard Perley outside his tent at A-96 Toul/Ochey, wearing a ribbon for '150 early morning missions'. (Richard Perley)

Above right: Ground crewmen replenish the magazines of a 50th Fighter Group P-47 at A-69. The eight 'point fifties' proved highly effective in ground strafing actions, the maximum 3,400 rounds capable of being dispensed in 35 seconds of short bursts. (Richard Perley)

Left: Although the prospect of a bale-out over water was remote when 9th Air Force fighter units were in eastern France, pilots still wore a Mae West life preserver under their parachute harness. There was also little requirement for oxygen on most missions, but the mask gave protection against fire, as did goggles. Here Lieutenant Perley appears to be wearing a British helmet. (Richard Perley)

Above: Lieutenant Richard
Perley and his personal
Thunderbolt, *Kandy K II.*
(Richard Perley)

Left: Captain Philip M.
Savides in front of his
personal P-47, *Juicy Lucy*,
at Toul/Ochey, autumn
1944. (Philip Savides)

61st
TROOP CARRIER GROUP

14th, 15th, 53rd and 59th Troop Carrier Squadrons

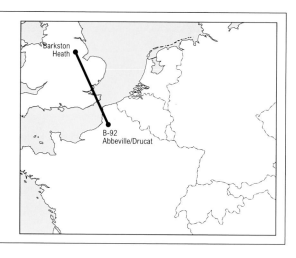

Left to right: 14th and 53rd Troop Carrier Squadron insignia.

67th
TACTICAL RECONNAISSANCE GROUP

12th, 15th, 107th and 109th Tactical Reconnaissance Squadrons; 30th and 33rd Photographic Reconnaissance Squadrons

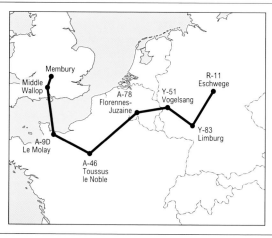

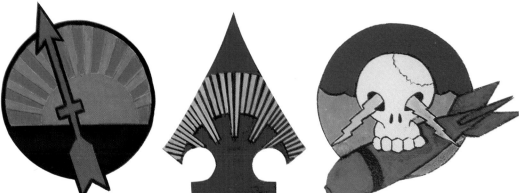

Left to right: 107th and 109th Tactical Reconnaissance Squadron insignia; and 33rd Photographic Reconnaissance Squadron insignia.

313th
TROOP CARRIER GROUP

29th, 47th, 48th, 49th Troop Carrier Squadrons

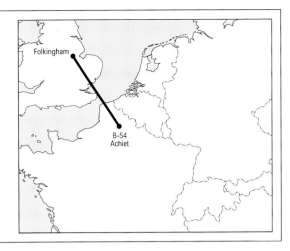

Right: C-47A 42-100646 was to have a long and eventful existence. Arriving in the United Kingdom in March 1944, it remained in Europe after hostilities, serving with a variety of units in the occupational air forces before going to Finland. After the Finns had operated the aircraft for 36 years, it was acquired by the Dutch Dakota Association and was still airworthy in 1995. In this photograph, taken at Nordholz in July 1945, '646' wears the nose code marking of the 47th TCS over the painted out 'L4' of the 91st TCS. (John Quincy)

Left: Taking off from Nordholz in July 1945, C-47A 42-100646 carries 'time expired' 406th Fighter Group personnel on the first stage of their journey home. (Stan Wyglendowski)

Right: The 313th TCG was the first IX TCC group to receive the C-46. During Operation 'Varsity', the airborne crossing of the Rhine on 24 March 1945, the group suffered the loss of sixteen of the 72 C-46s dispatched. A further forty were damaged and four of those were beyond economical repair. Thereafter the C-46 was withdrawn from combat operations as too vulnerable and fire-prone. The C-46D in the photograph, 44-77541 'N3-A', was badly damaged in an accident in April 1945. (USAAF)

314th
TROOP CARRIER GROUP

32nd, 50th, 61st and 62nd Troop Carrier Squadrons

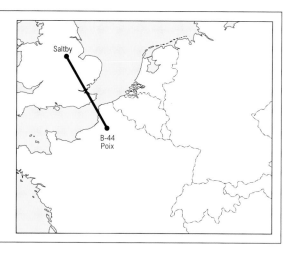

Above: Aircraft of the 61st and 62nd TCSs marshalled at Poix, France, for Operation 'Varsity', the Rhine crossing of 24 March 1945. (Via Dave Benfield)

Above: Another view of the line-up and early morning shadows. Douglas C-47 43-15326 of the 62nd TCS survived the war to serve in a civilian capacity as a DC-3 in Brazil for several years. It finally came to grief in a crash at Bhairawa on 5 November 1960 while serving with the Royal Nepal Airlines. (Via Dave Benfield)

Below: Preparations for towing CG-4A gliders for the Rhine crossing, 24 March 1945. The glider of the lead C-47 is in the foreground. The aircraft on the right, *Witch Hazel*, was the third aircraft to take off, piloted by 1/Lt Harold W. Wright. (Via Dave Benfield)

Above: Major Bennett Y. Allen, 314th Group Glider Officer and pilot of the first CG-4A to be towed from Poix for the Rhine crossing, talks with a 52nd TCW officer while awaiting take-off. (Via Dave Benfield)

Below: C-47 42-92862 'E5-R' strains to become airborne as men of the 32nd TCS watch take-offs at Poix for the 'Varsity' operation. (Via Dave Benfield)

315th
TROOP CARRIER GROUP

34th, 43rd, 309th and 310th Troop Carrier Squadrons

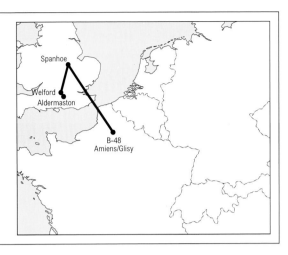

Right: The 315th TCG insignia (an actual jacket patch).

Above: A 309th TCS C-47 that suffered landing gear failure at Spanhoe. (Via Dave Benfield)

Below: Released British prisoners of war prepare to board C-47s of the 34th TCS at an airfield in Germany, May 1945. (Via William Brinson)

Above: Three members of 315th TCG Engineering at Spanhoe, England, display a variety of service clothes, autumn 1944. Captain Richard Bettis, Glider Engineering Officer, wears a B-10 intermediate jacket with muff. Sergeant Pappas, Engineering Clerk (with cycle), has an olive drab woollen sweater of non-military origin and Warrant Officer Robert Barnes, Assistant Group Engineering Officer, sports a light tan service jacket. Waco CG-4A gliders are in the background. The photograph was taken outside the Group Engineering Nissen hut. (William Brinson)

316th
TROOP CARRIER GROUP
36th, 37th, 44th and 45th Troop Carrier Squadrons

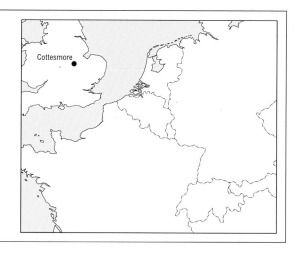

Below: Chaplain Willard arranged a party for orphans from Oakham on Christmas Day 1944. Here, shepherded by 316th personnel, the children wait for Father Christmas to arrive in a C-47. The photograph, taken from the control tower looking towards the eastern 'C' type hangar, also shows something of the freezing mists that took hold of north-west Europe at the end of 1944. (Via Dave Benfield)

Right: Father Christmas arrives and receives an enthusiastic greeting. (Via Dave Benfield)

Above right: An award ceremony at Cottesmore, England, in the winter of 1944–45. Despite being part of the 1st Allied Airborne Army, these officers still wear 9th Air Force patches. The rectan- gular RAF two-storey barracks in the background were erected early in the war. (Via Dave Benfield)

Below: Curtiss C-46D 44- 77686 of the 37th TCS draws a number of inter- ested spectators after putting down at Old Buckenham, England, one day in April 1945. Follow- ing the withdrawal of C-46s from combat operations, the other four groups of the 52nd Wing each received some six of these aircraft for use in transportation duties. The C-46 could carry nearly twice the load of a C- 47. (USAAF)

322nd
BOMBARDMENT GROUP

449th, 450th, 451st and 452nd Bombardment Squadrons

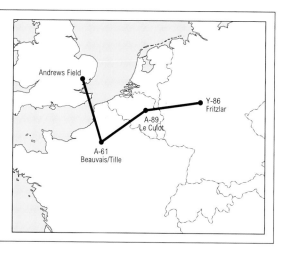

Above: *Clark's Little Pill* heads a column of 451st BS Marauders along the northern perimeter track at Andrews Field. This bomber suffered a fire in the right engine on Christmas Day 1944 when on its 155th combat mission. Lieutenant Maurice A. Neher and crew nursed the aircraft back to friendly territory, where the extent of the fire forced them to bale out. (USAAF)

Right: The venerable *Flak Bait*, the only aircraft of the Western Allies to complete more than 200 bombing sorties, stands on an airfield in Germany in the summer of 1945. Commencing combat operations in July 1943, the 449th BS aircraft completed its last, the 202nd, on 24 April 1945. (Clarence Luennemann)

Right: *Fightin Cock* entered combat in the summer of 1943 and had to undergo major repairs after being badly flak-damaged on 20 March 1944. On 12 August that year it again suffered flak damage, which disabled the hydraulic system. Forced to belly-land at Andrews Field, the Marauder skidded off the runway and hit the control tower, both the pilot and the co-pilot being killed in the collision. (USAAF)

Left: The record on *Flak Bait*. (Ian Mctaggart)

323rd
BOMBARDMENT GROUP

453rd, 454th 455th and 456th Bombardment Squadrons

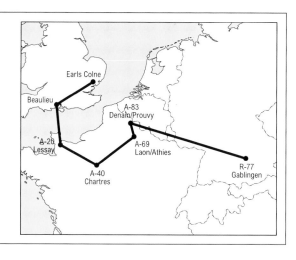

Left: S/Sgt Frank E. Mancuso, 1/Lt Clarence A. Hayden and S/Sgt Billy Pritchard pose in front of a Marauder named in honour of the United Services Organization, which, outside the USA, was primarily responsible for sponsoring show business entertainment for service-men. *U.S.O.* had its finale on 10 June 1944 when a direct hit by a shell knocked off the right engine. Pilot 2/Lt Harry A. Brown was able to make a belly-landing in a wheat field in the British sector of the Normandy beach-head. All the crew-men escaped without serious injury and were returned to England by LST (landing craft) the same day. British troops made good use of the Marauder's 'point-fifty' machine guns. (Frank Mancuso)

Right: On 15 May 1944 *Bingo Buster* was the first 323rd BG aircraft to complete 100 combat missions. Thereafter 9th Air Force HQ arranged for its return to the United States on a bond and morale-raising tour and *Bingo Buster* left the United Kingdom on D-Day, 6 June. The crew chief at Earls Colne airfield who cared for this record breaker was T/Sgt Wendell G. Polansky. (Mrs C. Hayden)

Left: *Mission Belle*, the second 323rd BG Marauder to survive 100 missions. (Mrs C. Hayden)

Right: *Lucky Cracki*, alias *Rock Hill Special*, flew its first mission on 28 July 1943, reached its 100th on 10 June 1944 and flew its last, the 184th, on 25 April 1945. No other B-26 in the 323rd BG had such an outstanding record of combat longevity. (Glenn Boone)

Right: When Colonel Carl R. Storrie moved from the 387th BG at Chipping Ongar to take command of the 98th Bomb Wing at Earls Colne he took his personal B-26 with him. *Bat-outa-hell II* had flown 22 missions with the 387th and when this photograph was taken had added another 34 with the 323rd BG, who placed the aircraft in the 455th BS for servicing. It survived hostilities with a total 144 missions completed. (John Moench)

Left, upper: B-26s taxying in after a mission. The mud at Laon was frozen hard on this December day. (George Spradling)

Left, lower: Sergeant John W. Daily, assistant crew chief of *Flaming Mamie*, works on an engine. The B-26B in the background is another veteran, *Punching Bag*, which went on to take part in more than 140 operations. (George Spradling)

Below: 2/Lt William Phelan (co-pilot), S/Sgt Thomas D. Jimmerson (crew chief) and 1/Lt

George Spradling with *Flaming Mamie* at Laon, December 1944. This B-26C failed to return from a

mission with another crew on 25 February 1945, falling victim to flak over Cologne.

Above: A Marauder airborne from Beaulieu for a mission in August 1944.

Right: *Flaming Mamie* taxies in at Laon after a mission in December 1944. (George Spradling)

Right: T/Sgt Roland 'Waddy' Somers (toggelier) and Lieutenant George Spradling (pilot) in the cockpit of *Flaming Mamie* at Laon, France, December 1944. Spradling completed 65 missions, the usual tour for 9th AF bomber crewmen. (George Spradling)

Left: *Crew 13* evidently faced up to superstition and gave their Marauder this tag. Here being towed to its dispersal point after making a single-engine landing at Laon in December 1944, the aircraft went on to survive the war with more than 150 missions to its credit. (George Spradling)

Right: Line-up on the Laon taxi track: 323rd Bomb Group Marauders stand ready for a mission. The aircraft in the foreground, *Mission Belle*, had one of the best records in the group and had flown its first mission on 16 July 1943 with the group's combat début. On 26 December 1944, a few days after this photograph was taken, the aircraft, on its 149th mission, had just unloaded its bombs on the target when it took a direct flak hit between an engine and the fuselage. (George Spradling)

Below: *Flaming Mamie* taxies by for another mission during the period of crisis that came to be known as the Battle of the Bulge. Freezing mist presented a pretty scene but made for perilous flying conditions. (George Spradling)

Below right: *The Jockey Club*, as its four officer tenants dubbed it, in the grip of winter snows, December 1944. Every tent had its log pile and the woods around Laon were severely depleted by the following spring.

344th
BOMBARDMENT GROUP

494th, 495th, 496th and 497th Bombardment Squadrons

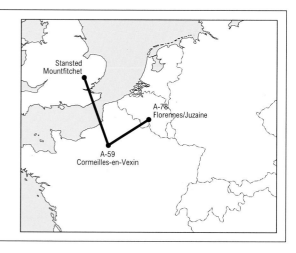

Right: A quiet moment on a 497th BS dispersal area near the control tower at Stansted, looking north-east towards the control tower (hidden by the B-26 on the left). A 1,000lb GP bomb lies in the foreground. The Marauder on the right is a B-26F model, which featured a higher angle of incidence to the wing. (George Kammermeyer)

Far right, top: Flak damaged the landing gear of *Shopworn Angel* on its twelfth mission, 21 April 1944, causing this collapse when Captain Lucius E. Clay, 495th BS Operations Officer, put down at Stansted. The crew were unhurt and the aircraft was repaired. *Shopworn Angel* was normally Lieutenant W. J. Woodrum's aircraft but he was in London on leave that day. The aircraft returned to operations in July 1944, only to become a victim of flak on St Valentine's Day 1945. (Jack Havener)

Above: Resplendent in freshly applied 'D-Day stripes', B-26 Marauders of the 344th Bomb Group assemble for a mission, June 1944. As the first group to arrive in the United Kingdom with Marauders, devoid of much camouflage paintwork, the 344th was known as 'The Silver Streaks'. (George Kammermeyer)

Below: Captain John Catlin, pilot of *100 Proof*, takes a look at his lucky escape—a hole made by an 88mm shell which had gone clean through the wing without exploding (probably because of a defective fuse). (George Kammermeyer)

Right: Lieutenant George Kammermeyer outside his Nissen hut billet in the 497th BS area with his British bicycle. These machines were issued to aircrew for personal transportation around the base, the outlying domestic sites being half a mile from the airfield. George paid a local cycle shop to fit a used three-speed rear wheel to improve performance—and thus began his lifelong addiction to cycling! (George Kammermeyer)

Above left: The lead box of the 344th heading for a target, summer 1944. A few minutes before this photograph was taken a shell splinter had cracked the Plexiglas in front of the co-pilot. (Jack Havener)

Left: Marauders of the 495th BS moving along Stansted's north-western perimeter track to take off on runway 12, April 1944. The deep vehicle tracks are evidence of spring rains, although going 'off the hard' was expressly forbidden other than in an emergency. (Jack Havener)

Above: A convoy off Weymouth prepares for the Normandy invasion. The photograph was taken after a mission to bomb a bridge at Corcelles-Seine on 4 June 1944. (George Kammermeyer)

Right: Veteran B-26B *Rosie O'Brady* and B-26F *Lak a Nookie* on the south-east end of the 5,500ft long concrete runway at A-59. Both aircraft survived to VE-Day. (Jack Havener)

Left: Marauders of the 344th taxying for take-off at undulating Cormeilles, spring 1945. The village of Genicourt is on the rising ground beyond the airfield. This was formerly a much-bombed Luftwaffe base.

Left: A. J. Frieburger's *Rum Buggy* at Stansted in April 1944. This Marauder was often out of commission but it survived the war. (Jack Havener)

Right: *Tom's Tantalizer* at Steeple Morden, England, spring 1945. A crew member has hung his parachute on the nosewheel door. This B-26B was badly damaged on 11 September 1944, repairs took several weeks and the aircraft was not returned to combat until January 1945. (Cal Sloan)

Right: Chow line at Cormeilles-en-Vexin for crews after returning from a mission in November 1944. No mess hall was available and food was prepared in field kitchens. A wrecked Luftwaffe hangar is seen in the background. The man facing the camera is S/Sgt Wojack, who was responsible for much of the nose art on 497th BS aircraft. (Jack Havener)

Above: *Facsimile* photographed at Stansted in April 1944. The pilot was Captain Harvey Johnson. The Marauder went missing in action on 27 April 1944. (Jack Havener)

Left: *The Buzzard* on a bright spring day at Stansted. Badly damaged on 9 August 1944, this aircraft was transferred to the 387th BG after repair. (Jack Havener)

Right: A shamrock hides this young lady's modesty on Captain Richard Hynes' *My Colleen*. The bomber took a beating from flak on 7 June 1944 and when 'Father' Hynes put it down at Stansted the landing gear collapsed. (Jack Havener)

Below: The origin of the name on Captain Maffry's B-26 was its part olive drab and part natural metal finish. During the 344th's movement from the United States to Great Britain there was a bad-weather delay in North Africa. To pass the time many of the crews began removing the camouflage paint from their aircraft and in most cases the task was not completed before they flew on to England. The comment 'The wings are coming by ATC' refers to the B-26's supposed lack of wing area. *Maffry's Mottled Marauder* flew over 140 missions before running out of fuel and being bellied-in by its pilot sixteen miles north-west of Charleroi, France, on 3 March 1945. (Jack Havener)

Right: *The Hearse III* was the macabre name given to Lieutenant W. Young's Marauder at Stansted. Severely flak damaged on 13 May 1944, it was transferred to the 322nd BG the following September. On 28 November 1944 it was again badly flak damaged and on reaching Allied territory the crew baled out—except for the pilot, who was killed when the aircraft crashed. (Jack Havener)

Below: *Six Hits and a Miss*, named after a popular vocal group of the time, was appropriate because of the six-man crew of a Marauder and the painting of a pin-up girl on its nose. (Jack Havener)

Right, upper: Lieutenant B. W. Seth was the original pilot of *Mary Ann* at Stansted. The aircraft was still going strong on VE-Day with more than 100 completed operations to its credit. (Jack Havener)

Right, lower: Another B-26B scraped of paint with the object of improving its performance was later named *You Cawn't Miss It* by Lieutenant J. R. Ashberry and crew; the name derived from the British habit of ending given directions with this phrase. The aircraft suffered severe battle damage on 3 September 1944 and landed at an Allied base on the Continent, never to return to the 344th. (Jack Havener)

Left, upper: Captain E. Schifani's *Bunny's Honey* carries an honest mission record. The duck symbol is for a diversion, the three donuts (doughnuts) are for recalled missions and the nine candy canes are for operations completed but where no bombs were dropped. Stansted's No 1

hangar can be seen in the distance. (Jack Havener)

Left, lower: The eye-catching, shapely nude on Lieutenant Witherbee's *Valkyrie* was a popular subject for GI cameras. This Marauder endured until 28 January 1945 when an engine failed on take-off

from Cormeilles, causing a crash and fire. (Jack Havener)

Above: Hydraulic fluid can be seen dripping over the nosewheel of *Yo-Yo Champ*, suggesting a rough landing. The nickname was a piece of fun poked at the pilot, Lieutenant A. J. Wood, who

was chubby and red-headed and known as 'Little Chicken', after the character in the children's story. With over 100 missions to its credit, *Yo-Yo Champ* was transferred to the 17th BG and shot down by Me 262 jets on 24 April 1945. (Jack Havener)

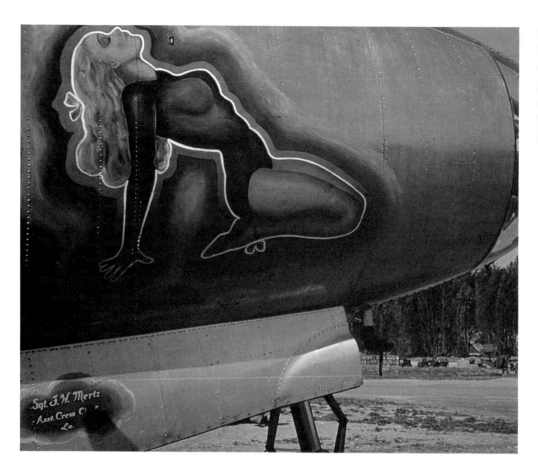

Right: Lieutenant W. R. Kolberg's *Piccadilly Willy*, with 25 missions up, at Stansted. This B-26B had well over 100 to its credit by the end of hostilities. (Jack Havener)

Above: This flamboyant girl was the illustration for *Smilin' Joy II*, whose original pilot was Lieutenant S. J. Robertson. Ground crew members often painted their names on nosewheel doors, as in this case. (Jack Havener)

Right: The name *Rosie O'Brady* was a pun on the well-known melody, the aircraft's original pilot being Lieutenant W. D. Brady. This aircraft was another veteran that endured to VE-Day, with over 140 operations to its credit. (Jack Havener)

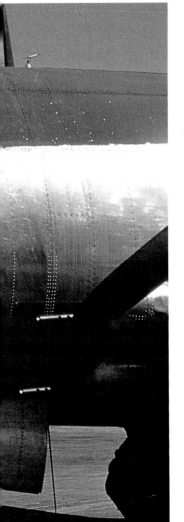

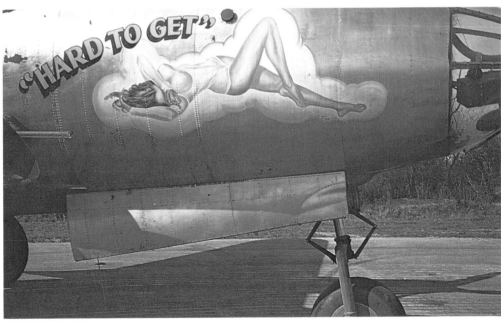

Above: The beautiful artwork on 497th BS CO Major D. D. Bentley's *Hard To Get*. Photographed here at Stansted in July 1944, the aircraft survived hostilities with 115 missions to its credit. (Jack Havener)

Left: The coffee connection was an obvious choice for Captain Jewel Maxwell. This is the second *Maxwell House*, the first being lost with its crew in April 1944. The plate on the Plexiglas nosepiece is where a fixed 'point-fifty' gun was situated, the weapon being removed from 9th Air Force B-26s. (Jack Havener)

Below: Lieutenant J. W. Scott's *Let'hal Lady*, with 82 missions up on its scoreboard. Forty more had been added by 16 April 1945 when flak caused the aircraft's demise. (Jack Havener)

Above: Lieutenant Jack Havener, with a finger in the hole made by a flak fragment that also struck the instruments in front of his co-pilot's position. This occurred during an attack on a V-1 site at Heuringhem, near St Omer, on 23 April 1944. (Jack Havener)

Left: *You've 'Ad It*. Lieutenant Harrison and crew used this frequently heard British expression—meaning that something was not available—as a name for their aircraft. The admirer is Lieutenant Havener. (Jack Havener)

Above: *Johnny Come Lately* was named after the original pilot, Lieutenant John Nemeth, although this photograph was taken long after he had finished his tour and returned to the States. The aircraft had 125 missions when, in March 1945, Captain John K. Havener, like most 'Johns' in the group, posed by this appropriately named aircraft (which he had piloted) shortly before leaving France and returning to the USA. (Jack Havener)

Right: Naked and unashamed: B-26F 43-34568 'K9-Q' of the 494th BS on a rain-soaked airfield in Germany, spring 1945. (Ralph Woolner)

Right: The incongruous occupant of an English hedgerow. Jocko, the 497th BS's unofficial mascot, was owned by Lieutenant Joe Lane, co-pilot of *Smilin' Joy*. He bought it from a C-47 crew that had purchased the male monkey in West Africa but by the time they reached St Mawgan, Cornwall, had decided that it was too much trouble to care for and were pleased to transfer the animal to Joe. Jack Havener of the 497th BS recalls: 'Many brave flight crew souls took turns baby-sitting Jocko while Joe was flying missions or on leave, but eventually he became too much to handle and one of the enlisted men in the ground echelon took over the duties. Our flight surgeon gave Jocko vitamins to help him survive the English damp . . . and he eventually went home with Joe in September, smuggled out in a barracks bag. We learned later that Joe's wife divorced him and we all surmised it was because of that damned monkey!' (Jack Havener)

354th
FIGHTER GROUP

353rd, 355th and 356th Fighter Squadrons

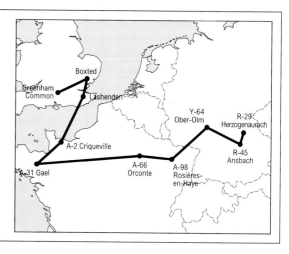

Right: A 353rd FS P-51B is prepared for spark plug changing on a Boxted hardstand, January 1944. Because of the lean fuel mixtures used to extend the aircraft's range, plugs had to be inspected after every mission of long duration—a time-consuming task for ground crews. (USAAF)

Left: A mock briefing in the Operations Building at Boxted, 25 January 1944. The call-signs and target data are bogus, the scene being set up for the camera. Colonel Kenneth Martin, the Group CO, stands on the right. Interestingly, security has lapsed in overlooking the plan of Boxted airfield and the location of the three squadrons' aircraft dispersals. The gas-proof, reinforced concrete building is still intact today, in use as a fireworks store. (AFM)

Above: Lieutenant-Colonel James H. Howard, CO of the 356th FS, in his personal P-51B, posing with its crew chief, S/Sgt Marcus Hanson, at Boxted on 25 January 1944 shortly after Howard had received this aircraft. While flying another Mustang on 11 January 1944, Howard single-handedly broke up an enemy fighter attack on a B-17 formation. For this action he was awarded the only Medal of Honor won by a US fighter pilot flying in the European Theatre of Operations. The Japanese symbols on the Mustang were for his victories claimed while flying in the Burma/China theatre the previous year. (USAAF)

Above: In December 1943 P-51Bs of the 354th FG visited most combat bases in England in order to familiarize personnel with the Mustang. This was aimed at avoiding misiden- tification, there being a prevalent misconception that any single-engine fighter with square-cut wing tips was an Me 109. *Bonnie B*, photographed while visiting the B-17 base at Podington, was the personal Mustang of 353rd FS pilot Lieutenant Donald M. Beerbower, who was credited with 15$\frac{1}{2}$ aerial victories before being killed in action on 7 July 1944. This 'score' was surpassed by only one other 9th Air Force pilot. (William Furniss)

Right: Good use is made of an intact Luftwaffe hangar at R-29 by the 356th FS. (Via Steve Sheflin)

Left: A Mustang of the 355th Fighter Squadron being serviced on a hardstanding near Lodge Lane at Boxted airfield, January 1944. The early P-51Bs were plagued by coolant leaks caused by high-altitude operations. (USAAF)

358th
FIGHTER GROUP

365th, 366th and 367th Fighter Squadrons

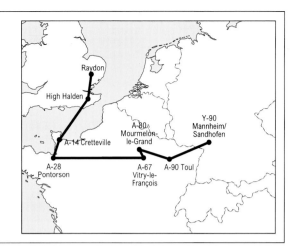

Above. left to right:
358th FG insignia; and 365th, 366th and 367th FS insignia.

Left: S/Sgt Buffington and S/Sgt Lebbertus Lok work on a 365th FS P-47D at Mannheim/Sandhofen, May 1945. The 365th had a white cowling band in addition to the 'CH' squadron identification letters. (Via Robert Bowen)

Right: S/Sgt Rubitchek talks to Lieutenant Davis in his colourful *Tarheel Hal*, a late-model P-47D of the 366th FS. The red nose, common to most aircraft of the 1st TAF, was backed by the squadron's yellow cowling band and that in turn was bordered with blue and white chequers on the cowling flap. The dark blue star-spangled decoration was a purely personal adornment, as was the red, white and blue rudder trim tab in the group's orange tail marking. (Via Robert Bowen)

Above: Captain Hall waits in the cockpit while P-47D 42-28928 is refuelled by S/Sgt DeFloria and Corporal Waller. The 367th FS red noseband amounted to a continuation of the 1st TAF nose marking; the orange tail was devised and implemented by the group as a distinguishing marking in the winter of 1944–45. (Via Robert Bowen)

Right: Members of the 358th FG pose with a Nazi flag retrieved from the Nuremberg stadium by men of the 45th Infantry Division and presented to the 358th with the comment 'Use it for engine rags or some other useful purpose'. Seen here (left to right) are Major Robert J. Bell, CO of the 462nd Air Service Squadron (which provided maintenance support for the group's aircraft); Sergeant Conn of the same organization; Colonel James B. Tipton, CO of the 358th Fighter Group at Sandhofen; and M/Sgt Ross of 358th HQ. (Via Robert Bowen)

362nd
FIGHTER GROUP

377th, 378th and 379th Fighter Squadrons

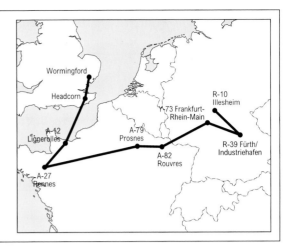

Right: Lieutenant-Colonel Joe Laughlin's second P-47D, named *Five by Five*, with crew chief Sergeant J. R. Chodor and armourer Corporal George Atkinson. This Thunderbolt was carrying 42 'sortie completed' symbols when this photograph was taken at Headcorn, Kent. (Via Chuck Mann)

Left: Lieutenant Kenneth Kitts' personal P-47D was looked after by Sergeant Otis Kimmons and his men in the 379th FS at Wormingford. Kitts was killed while strafing on 8 April 1944. The artwork on the cowling of *Loko* was, like that on most of the original aircraft of the squadron, painted by Captain George Rarey, a former commercial artist; also a combat pilot, he was killed in action on 27 June 1944. (Chuck Mann)

Right: In August 1944 Joe Laughlin became CO of the 362nd FG. In this photograph, taken in September 1944 at Prosnes, he is seen, cigar in mouth, with his pet spaniel Prince. The scoreboard on the side of his new P-47D-25 Thunderbolt has a warship symbol for a cruiser sunk in Brest harbour on 25 August 1944. (Chuck Mann)

Left: The insignia on Captain John Shumway's *Betty* at Wormingford, March 1944. The crew chief was Sergeant Dan Salzman. (Chuck Mann)

Right: *Wheel Boy* was Lieutenant Ken McCleary's Thunderbolt. He was shot down and taken prisoner in June 1944. The aircraft's crew chief was Sergeant William Marles. (Chuck Mann)

Left: The insignia on Lieutenant Thurman Morrison's *Memphis Rebel II.* (Chuck Mann)

Right: *The Deacon*, Lieutenant Gordon Larsen's aircraft. He was shot down in August 1944 but evaded capture and returned to Allied lines. (Chuck Mann)

Left: *Bucephalus II*, named after Alexander the Great's famous charger, was the mount of Lieutenant Clough Gee and groomed by Sergeant Al Cutrone. Gee was shot down and killed by an FW 190 on 7 June 1944; his was one of five 362nd FG Thunderbolts lost that day. (Chuck Mann)

Left: *Trishie*, alias *The Tired Eagle*: pilot Lieutenant Ray Fuchs, crew chief Sergeant William Faulkner. (Chuck Mann)

Below: A flight of yellow-nose, 379th FS P-47s peels off high over Germany in the spring of 1945. The 362nd Group identification marking was a red top to the fin. (Chuck Mann)

Left: *Danny Boy*—pilot Lieutenant Robert McKee, crew chief Sergeant Jack Farbman—photographed at Headcorn, spring 1944. (Chuck Mann)

Right: A distant formation of 362nd FG Thunderbolts high over Germany, spring 1945. (Chuck Mann)

Left: A caricature of the group commander and his aircraft, which carried a chequerboard cowling in squadron colours. This painting, the work of Joe Carpenter, is seen displayed at Straubing in Germany in May 1945. (Chuck Mann)

363rd
FIGHTER GROUP/TACTICAL RECONNAISSANCE GROUP

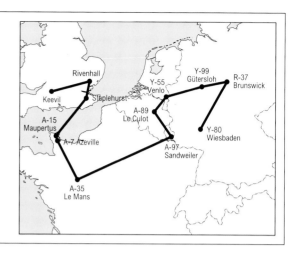

380th Fighter Squadron/160th Tactical Reconnaissance Squadron, 381st Fighter Squadron/161st Tactical Reconnaissance Squadron and 382nd Fighter Squadron/162nd Tactical Reconnaissance Squadron

Below: *Joan V,* an F-6D of the 161st TRS, photographed at Asch, Belgium, in the autumn of 1944, has an oblique-angle camera installed in the rear fuselage near the national insignia. (Stan Wyglendowski)

365th
FIGHTER GROUP

386th, 387th and 388th Fighter Squadrons

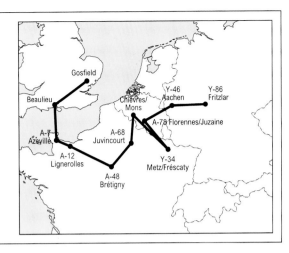

Below: Captain Zell Smith, of the 388th FS, 'checks his tail' in P-47 'C4-Z' at A-84 Chièvres, November 1944. This was Smith's fourth 'C4-Z'. Two were so battle-damaged they had to be salvaged and one was shot down while being flown by another pilot, but the fourth, 42-28669, saw out the war. Smith was credited with shooting down two FW 190s on 21 October 1944. (D. K. Beaumeister via Zell Smith)

366th
FIGHTER GROUP

389th, 390th and 391st Fighter Squadrons

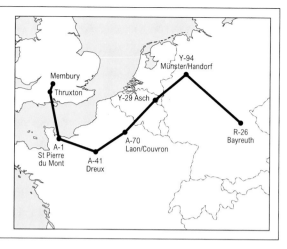

Right: The Group Commander's Thunderbolt in the snow at Asch, Belgium. Harold N. Holt selected this P-47D, 42-76516, as his personal mount in February 1944 when he was CO of the 390th FS and flew it until the end of hostilities. During these thirteen months of operations *Magic Carpet* made 175 sorties with Holt and other pilots and not once had to be turned back through mechanical problems—an outstanding record for a P-47. (Col. Harry Holt)

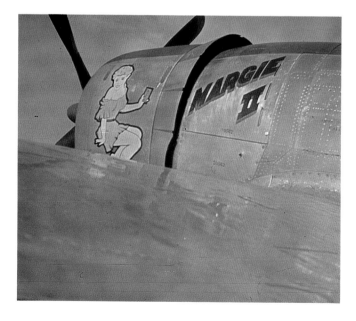

Left: *Margie II* was Captain Lee O. Rorex's usual mount in the 389th FS. (John Meyer)

Left: *Sissy Mine*, alias *My Aching Back*, of the 389th FS at Münster. (John Meyer)

Right: Lieutenant Purdy's P-47D *Heartless Helen*, with a impressive record of fighter-bomber sorties. The aircraft was photographed at Münster/Handorf in the spring of 1945. The marks on the leading edge of the wing were for sighting purposes. (John Meyer)

Left: Lieutenant Robert Blaker's *Tulsa Traveler* at Münster/Handorf, spring 1945. (John Meyer)

367th
FIGHTER GROUP

392nd, 393rd and 394th Fighter Squadrons

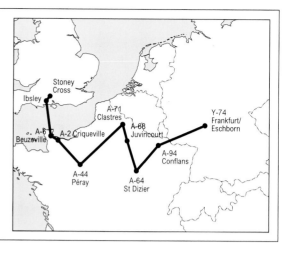

Left: Four 392 FS pilots at A-68 Juvincourt, France— Ed Haskamp, James C. Paschell, James C. Fincher and Clark Livingston. All survived combat. (Via Jack Curtis)

Right: A distinctive 'face' on the nose of P-38J *Freda*. Yellow was the 394th FS's identifying colour. (W. Furniss)

Left: *Freda* taxies out for take-off at Podington, England, August 1944. (W. Furniss)

Right: 'Doc' Livingston poses with his aircraft. (Via Jack Curtis)

Below: Ground crews with Lieutenant Gerald O'Donnell's *Lucky Irish*, which sports three victory symbols (of which one is a shared aerial victory). This Lightning was lost with another pilot on 23 December 1944. (Via Jack Curtis)

Left: *Little Buckarroo* was the personal aircraft of Major Robert ('Buck') Rogers. When this photograph was taken at Clastres on 12 October 1944, the P-38 had 36 combat sorties to its credit and five enemy aircraft claimed in ground strafing attacks. (Via Jack Curtis)

Below: Lieutenant Horrace Hartwig and crew chief by his P-38J. The aircraft, prepared for combat, has a 500lb bomb on each wing rack. (Via Jack Curtis)

Left: Lieutenant Jimmy Paschell and his *Viking 2* at Clastres, October 1944. The ground crew often named individual engines on multi-engine aircraft: here the left engine is named *Minnie* and the right *Elva*. (Via Jack Curtis)

Right: Refuelling Lieutenant Ken B. Jorgensen's 394th FS Lightning '4N-J' in Normandy. The 367th's three squadrons were placed on separate advanced landing grounds when the group first moved to France. The 394th were operating from A-6, Ste Mère-Église, where this photograph was taken. (Via Jack Curtis)

Right: Lieutenant Clark ('Doc') Livingston's aircraft. The victory symbols are for two FW 190s claimed destroyed on 25 August 1944. The red nose tip was a 392nd FS identity marking. (Via Jack Curtis)

Left: Crew chief Sergeant F. P. Pecora and his assistant in front of Lieutenant Sam Plotecia's P-38 *Kozy Koza* at Clastres, October 1944. (Via Jack Curtis)

Above: A 393rd FS bomb service trailer serving as a carriage for an almost intact V-1 flying bomb, found near Mourmelon-le-Grand and destined to be transported to the USA for evaluation. (John Quincy)

Left: Insignia of the 394th Fighter Squadron.

Right: The showy nose decorations of Major C. F. Matheson's Philbert V, a 394th FS P-47D. The aircraft was photographed at Fürth, spring 1945. (Ralph Woolner)

Below: The immaculate *Philbert V* against a background of ex-Luftwaffe buildings at Fürth. The red warning arrow is on a building, not the Thunderbolt! (Ralph Woolner)

368th
FIGHTER GROUP

395th, 396th and 397th Fighter Squadrons

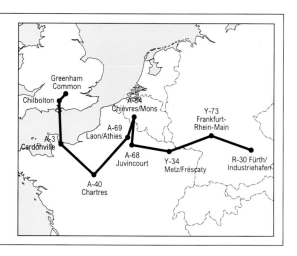

Below: The Thunderbolt could take severe damage and still keep flying. The 395th FS pilot of *Sleepy Jean the 3rd* managed to make a successful landing at St Dizier despite the twisted propeller blade. (Ralph Woolner)

Right: Captain George McWilliams flying a P-47D against a background of the Bavarian Alps, summer 1945. The yellow tail tip was the group marking of the 368th. (Arthur Houston)

Above: *Dirtybut III* at R-68 Straubing, Germany, summer 1945. At this time many low-hour P-47s had been transferred from other groups, that in the background still retaining its 373rd FG code markings. (Arthur Houston)

Right: The dented engine cowling of *Sleepy Jean the 3rd*. (Ralph Woolner)

370th
FIGHTER GROUP

401st, 402nd and 485th Fighter Squadrons

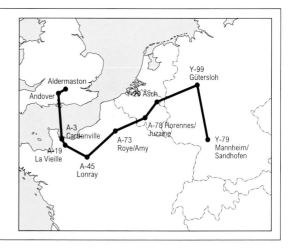

Above: A blue and red spinner backed by a red cowling band was the unit marking carried by the 485th Fighter Squadron on its Lightnings. *Spirit of Oak Ridge* had a field application of olive drab paint on the upper surfaces to make it less conspicuous when parked on forward landing strips.

371st
FIGHTER GROUP

404th, 405th and 406th Fighter Squadrons

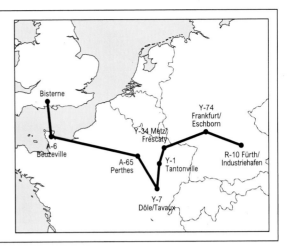

Right: Although coloured noses identified its squadrons, the 371st FG never adopted a distinguishing tail marking, although a great many of its aircraft carried alternating blue and unpainted engine cowling flaps. This 406th FS P-47D, 44-20097, '4W-E' was photographed at Fürth, Germany. (Link Derick)

Left: A red cowling identified the 404th FS. P-47D 44-20284 '9Q-O' had previously served with the 367th FG, whose tail colours had yet to be removed when this photograph was taken at Fürth in the spring of 1945. (Link Derick)

373rd
FIGHTER GROUP

410th, 411th and 412th Fighter Squadrons

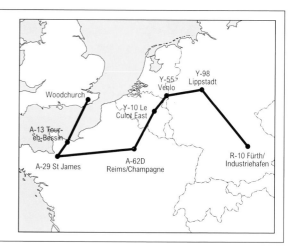

Above: : *Dorothy K*, the personal Thunderbolt of Captain Talmadge Ambrose, seen at Y-98 Lippstadt, Germany. This aircraft carries nine victory symbols, four of which were aerial victories obtained on 8 April 1945 when the 410th FS was credited with shooting down twelve FW 190Ds in a mêlée near Hanover. Two 373rd FG aircraft were lost. The blue tail tip was a group identification marking adopted by the 373rd late in the war. (Talmadge Ambrose)

386th
BOMBARDMENT GROUP

552nd, 553rd, 554th and 555th Bombardment Squadrons

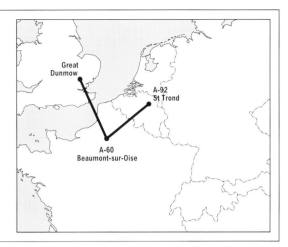

Above: The crew of *Geronimo* on the bomber's completion of 75 missions, for many of which Captain Ralph Marble piloted the aircraft. Battle damage and wear and tear eventually took their toll and the aircraft was declared unfit for further service on 27 August 1944 when it had completed 112 sorties. (USAAF)

Above: *Sexy Betsy* on its dispersal at Great Dunmow, summer 1944. The aircraft served with the 386th from February 1944 until its transfer to the 394th BG before the end of the war. (Richard Denison)

Right: Armourers of the 554th BS fixing the fins of 500lb GP bombs before installation on *Mert and the Flying Circus*. (USAAF)

Above: A crew poses with *Mert and the Flying Circus* after its completion of 80 missions. Fourth from the left is Major Leland Perry, pilot and Squadron CO; kneeling are Captain Thomas B. Haire, the Group Intelligence Officer, and the crew chief. After sustaining heavy battle damage in July 1944 this aircraft was assigned to the 344th BG after repair but was scrapped in September 1944. (USAAF)

Above: High over Germany, *Spare Parts* comes home from another mission. The photograph was evidently taken in the latter part of 1944 as the so-called invasion stripes on the wings have been painted out. (John Meyers)

Above right: B-26B 42-96128 was the last Marauder from Baltimore production with a complete camouflage finish; thereafter they came either completely naked in shiny metal or with just the upper surfaces painted dark green. (John Meyers)

Right: *Dinah Might* heading home to Great Dunmow over the Channel with flak perforations in her tail. An original combat aircraft of the group, it had its share of battle repairs, including a new rudder. The ground crew were apparently too busy to get round to updating the wing insignia with white bars. *Dinah Might* did not return from bombing a storage depot at St Wendle on 18 November 1944, on what is believed to have been its 129th mission. (John Meyers)

Right: *Hard Luck*, with 80 missions up and still going strong, at Beaumont-sur-Oise, October 1944. This bomber, later transferred to the 397th BG, amassed a total of 164 missions by the end of the war. (John Meyers)

Left: A flight of B-26s returning from a mission in the autumn of 1944. 'YA-O' was named *Ole Gray Mare* and 'YA-S' was *Dink's Dandy*. (Richard Denison)

Above: Lieutenant John Meyers poses by the 'beat-up' tail of old *Hard Luck*, a veteran B-26B of the 553rd BS, at Beaumont-sur-Oise, France, in October 1944. (John Meyers)

Above: Two Douglas A-26 Invaders on a combat trial mission in September 1944. The 553rd BS carried out such trials with the A-26 for a limited period during the summer of 1944 but the group did not convert to the type until the following year. (John Meyers)

Left: Cold fingers! Sergeant Crowman services the starboard propeller mechanism of *La Paloma* on a bitter January day in 1945 at Beaumont-sur-Oise. (John Meyers)

Left: Tail gunner Sergeant R. H. Biby beside his post on a Beaumont-sur-Oise dispersal, October 1944. On 19 November, during a mission to bomb a defended village at Merode, the lead formation was met by an accurate flak barrage Nine of the fifteen B-26s were damaged, but the only casualties were in *Spare Parts*, one crewman being wounded and Sergeant Biby killed. (John Meyers)

Below: B-26F *La Paloma* in January snow with its pilot, Lieutenant John Meyers. The principal difference between the B-26F and earlier models was the set of the wing relative to the fuselage, with the benefit of quicker lift on take-off. (John Meyers)

Above left: A-26s follow a B-26. The latter sighted on target for them: in the early trials no Invaders with bombardier nose compartments were available. This photo was taken from another A-26. (John Meyers)

Above: Spectacle in the heavens: a mass of contrails, viewed from an A-26 high over Germany. The beads of moisture are on the inside of the Plexiglas. (John Meyers)

Left: Invaders of the 553rd BS 'cab rank' for a mission at St Trond, Belgium, spring 1945. The group converted completely to the A-26 in February that year. (Richard Denison)

Right: A solid-nose A-26B, 43-22343, over Belgium in 1945. The pilots of this model released the bomb load on the visual signal of the lead aircraft of the formation. (Richard Denison)

Above: The cockpit of an A-26 Invader. The aircraft did not have a co-pilot, and with the solid-nose versions the crew numbered three in total. (John Meyers)

Right: A-26B 43-22341 warms up at St Trond. The 553rd BS painted the cowlings of its A-26s blue as an additional squadron marking. (Richard Denison)

Above: *Rat Poison Jr* was the 553rd BS's 'lead plane'. Major Stewart Marquis, Operations Officer, is in the cockpit and Lieutenant Richard Denison, Squadron Navigator, stands by the nose. Only the lead and deputy lead aircraft of an A-26 formation carried a navigator. (Richard Denison)

Left: Invader 'AN-O 'at rest in spring sunshine, St Trond, April 1945. The glazed-nose version of the Invader carried a navigator/ bombardier and this, the A-26C model, was used for group and squadron leads. A 552nd BS aircraft can be seen in the background in this photograph. (Richard Denison)

Below: The most distin-guished B-26 of the 386th BG, the original *Rat Poison* was a combat aircraft of the 553rd BS from the spring of 1943. Retained by the group as a standby after conversion to the A-26, the aircraft is seen here taxying at St Trond and displaying 164 'mission completed' symbols. (Richard Denison)

Above: Another view of *Rat Poison*. The original paint became so worn that it was resprayed in the spring of 1945. (Richard Denison)

Below: A view of Paris on VE-Day, 8 May 1945, taken from a 386th BG Invader. (John Meyers)

387th
BOMBARDMENT GROUP

556th, 557th, 558th and 559th Bombardment Squadrons

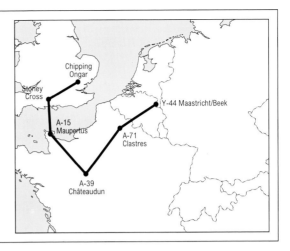

Below: Not so *Lucky Lady*, off the end of a Chipping Ongar runway on 25 May 1944. Taking off on the main runway for its 23rd mission, the aircraft suffered a complete instrument failure. It made a short circuit and Lieutenant Fisher landed fast on the east–west runway, a wing tip clipping the tail of another Marauder waiting on the perimeter track. *Lucky Lady* had previously served with the B-26 Pathfinder Squadron. (George Vasaumper)

Above: Shiny new *Top Sarge 2nd*, at around the time of its first mission on 25 May 1944. This B-26C went on to complete 101 missions by the war's end. The crew chief was Sergeant Gerard Goulet. (George Vasaumper)

Left: Luftwaffe fighters put an end to *Mississippi Mud Cat* on 23 December 1944, during its 150th mission. Six crew members managed to bale out but the pilot, Lieutenant Vernon Staub, was killed when the aircraft crashed. In this photograph, taken at Chipping Ongar in the summer of 1944, red propeller bosses identify it as with the 559th BS. (George Vasaumper)

Right: *Heavenly Body* (the name was painted on the other side of the nose) was originally the personal aircraft of the 558th BS CO, Major Joseph Richardson. On 8 June 1944, while on an evening mission to bomb a fuel dump in the Forêt de Grimbosq at 6,000ft in poor weather, the Marauder took a direct flak hit. No parachutes were seen. *Heavenly Body* was at the time on its 92nd mission. The crew chief was Sergeant Loyd Bucklew. (George Vasaumper)

Right: The name of this Marauder was based on a crew member's rendering of the common American saying 'rougher than a cob'. *Roughernacob* collected flak damage on its 111th mission on 12 August 1944, forcing Lieutenant Moriarty to crash-land on the Continent. (George Vasaumper)

Right and below: The original pilot of this aircraft, 1/Lt James E. Anderson, had an expectant wife and his concern was 'just her', expressed with an accent as 'jisther'—hence the nickname. The crew chief, T/Sgt George Vasaumper, stands beside the nose. The aircraft met an unusual end. It was taxying for its 95th mission at Stoney Cross when a flare gun in the cockpit fell out of its holster and fired. The flare went down the boot of the pilot, who, in agony, opened the top escape hatch and leapt out, straight into the left propeller. As the co-pilot was unable to work the brakes, *Jisther* went off the track and crashed into a hangar. (George Vasaumper)

Top: *Hangover Hut* on its hardstand at Chipping Ongar, May 1944, displaying 66 'mission completed' symbols. This bomber went on to fly a total of 151 missions by VE-Day. The man on the engine is believed to be the crew chief, T/Sgt Thomas F. Coughlin. (George Vasaumper)

Above: *The Big Hairy Bird* spent most of its operational life with the 397th BG, being transferred to the 558th BS, 387th BG, towards the end of hostilities. The nose decoration made this aircraft the prime candidate for the accolade of the most colourful Marauder in the 9th Air Force. (Alvaro Sousa)

391st
BOMBARDMENT GROUP

572nd, 573rd, 574th and 575th Bombardment Squadrons

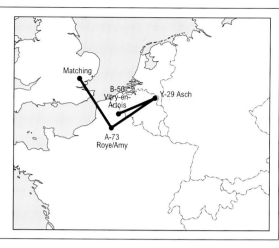

Left: B-26C 42-107620 of the 575th BS, bearing the yellow triangle that was the group identification marking of the 391st. (Via Bob Mynn)

Right: *Skyhag*, an original combat aircraft of the 574th BS, was one of sixteen 391st BG Marauders shot down on 23 December 1944. The formation of thirty-one B-26s had just bombed a rail bridge at Ahrweiler when it was attacked by several waves of Me 109s. This Battle of the Bulge action represented the highest loss suffered by a B-26 group on a single mission. (Via Bob Mynn)

Right: Crews board a 6 x 6 truck at the start of their journey to Coomb House, near Shaftesbury, for a few days' rest and recuperation. Most bomber crews were sent to one of the so-called 'flak homes' half way through their tour. (Via Bob Mynn)

Below: The 391st BG converted to the A-26 Invader at the end of March 1945. This aircraft of the 572nd BS was photographed at Nordholz, Germany, in May that year. (John Quincy via Stan Wyglendowski)

Left: A 'solid-nose' A-26B, 41-39588, at Nordholz. The A-26 was originally developed for low-level operations, hence the formidable forward-firing armament of eight .50-calibre machine guns in four under-wing packages and eight in the nose. (John Quincy via Stan Wyglendowski)

Below: A gas wagon with a trailer goes out to replenish Invaders of the 391st BG visiting Nordholz. The nearest aircraft, 43-22622 of the 572nd BS, is an A-26C. (John Quincy)

Left: A line-up of the 391st BG's new A-26s at Nordholz. Although beset with teething troubles, the A-26 proved to be an excellent combat aircraft. It utilized the same basic engines as the B-26 and had a similar bomb load capacity, but it had a much better performance by virtue of the comparative lightness, with a top speed nearly 100mph faster than that of the Marauder under certain conditions. (John Quincy)

394th
BOMBARDMENT GROUP

584th, 585th, 586th and 587th Bombardment Squadrons

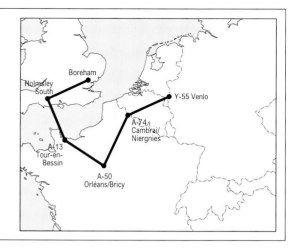

Above: B-26F 43-34373 '4T-F', operated by the 586th BS, seen after landing at Chièvres/Mons on a snowy day in January 1945. On the 29th of that month the aircraft attempted to take off for its fifth combat mission, but either turbulence or engine failure prevented it from becoming airborne and it crashed off the end of the runway. The co-pilot was killed and the pilot was seriously injured. (USAAF)

Above: Another view of B-26F 43-34373. (USAAF)

Left: As with most art on B-26s, that for *The Passionate Witch* was painted on the two steel panels positioned to afford protection to the pilot and his controls from ground fire during low-level attacks. The Marauder was rarely used for such work, but any means of warding off flak splinters was welcomed. (John Egan)

Above: Symbols denoting two decoy and 21 combat

missions completed on the A-2 flight jacket of 587th BS Captain Warren E. Buhler. 'Buzz' Buhler went on to fly a total of 65 combat missions, the standard tour for 9th Air Force bomber crewmen. The jacket is now held by the US Air Force Museum at Dayton, Ohio. (William Furness)

Left: *Thumper*, a B-26B of the 587th BS, rolls by Podington control tower, June 1944; the pilot is visiting his brother, a B-17 pilot. This aircraft was later transferred to the 1st Pathfinder Squadron and eventually salvaged in 1945. (William Furness)

Right: *Redlight Rosie*, a B-26B of the 587th BS, flew its first mission on 13 June 1944 and went on to complete 107 more by VE-Day. (John Egan)

Right: The artwork for Lieutenant William Drake's *The Draggin Lady* was based on the Dragon Lady cartoon character in the servicemen's *Stars and Stripes* newspaper strip 'Terry and the Pirates'. (John Egan)

397th
BOMBARDMENT GROUP

596th, 597th, 598th and 599th Bombardment Squadrons

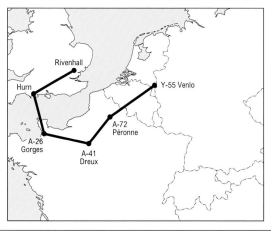

Right: Leaving a full-power oil and fuel-rich exhaust trail, a heavily loaded B-26 climbs away from A-72 Péronne, France, in February 1945. (Stan Walsh)

Right: *Dee Feater*, seen flying near Chelmsford in August 1944. (C. E. Brown)

Below: Bombs away! Eight 500lb bombs fall in train from 397th Marauders. One bomb straying will pick its own target! (Stan Walsh)

Left: B-26F *Helen Highwater III* of the 597th BS and *Kreihl's Cradle* of the 598th BS, on a combat mission in February 1945. (Stan Walsh)

Left: Poised for take-off: B-26G 44-67832 and B-26F 43-34335, both of the 598th BS, at Péronne in April 1945. (Stan Walsh)

Above: B-26 pilot Lieutenant Swenson examines an abandoned Luftwaffe 88mm anti-aircraft gun in a Magdeburg street. A few days earlier this gun was probably one of those that fired at his aircraft when he was bombing the nearby railway yards. (Stan Walsh)

Above: Famed for its distinctive nose decorations, *The Big Hairy Bird* of the 599th BS taxies out at Péronne on a cold January day. (Stan Walsh)

Right: A busty nude in a bikini against a background of a map of the USA was the embellishment on *The Milk Run Special*. Seen here at Steeple Morden, England, in the spring of 1945, this B-26 displays more than 100 mission symbols. (Cal Sloan)

Right: A view of *The Milk Run Special* from the starboard beam gun position of another B-26. (Stan Walsh)

404th
FIGHTER GROUP

506th, 507th and 508th Fighter Squadrons

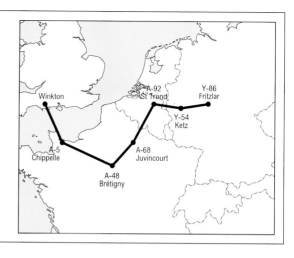

Below: In contrast to the bright colours adopted by most 9th Air Force fighter groups in the winter of 1944–45 to identify their aircraft, those of the 404th FG wore only the official unit codes. The 508th FS's P-47D 42-29140, here flying over Belgium in about March 1945, has two 'zero rail' air-to-ground rockets under each wing. The 404th FG was one of the first groups to receive this armament. (Leon Moon)

Above: During the Luftwaffe's mass formation raids on continental Allied airfields on New Year's Day 1945, a few disorganized FW 190As of II/JG 4 strafed St Trond. One, 'White 11', was slightly damaged by ground fire, whereupon its pilot, Gefreiter Walter Wagner, landed and was taken prisoner. The 404th FG immediately appropriated the Focke Wulf, painting it bright red overall and applying US insignia. The intention was to make the fighter airworthy, but it had to be left behind when the 404th moved on to another base and was still at St Trond in April 1945 when these photographs were taken. The 404th's humour is evident in the tail number, which is the date of the Focke Wulf's capture, and the code letters 'OO-L' ('Oh Oh Hell'). (Richard Denison)

405th
FIGHTER GROUP

509th, 510th and 511th Fighter Squadrons

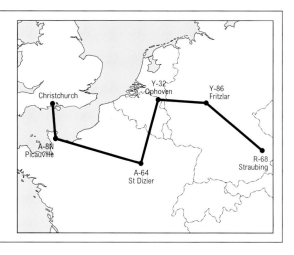

Left: Hauling two 500lb GP bombs under the wings, P-47 'G9-B' of the 509th FS takes off for a fighter-bomber mission from St Dizier, France, autumn 1944. (Ralph Woolner)

Right: The landing gear folds as another Thunderbolt sets out on a mission in late September 1944. This aircraft still retains the full black and white 'invasion stripes' round the fuselage, although the removal of those on the upper surfaces had been ordered in July. The ground crew was probably too busy with more vital tasks during summer's intensive period of fighter-bomber operations. (Ralph Woolner)

Right: The 405th FG had a unique means of distinguishing its aircraft by painting cockpit canopies in the appropriate squadron colours. This nearly new P-47D-28-RE model sports the 509th FS's red trim. (Ralph Woolner)

406th
FIGHTER GROUP

512th, 513th and 514th Fighter Squadrons

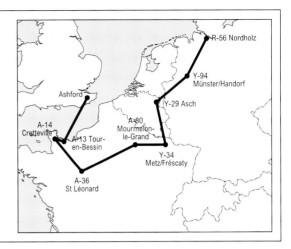

Above: Under evening cloud, a flight of P-47s returns to Ashford ALG, May 1944. (John Quincy)

Right: The 514th FS living area at Ashford. Air attack was expected and 'foxholes' were ordered to be dug. The 'pup tent' and covers were to keep rain from adding to the high water table. (John Quincy)

Left: It could be warm in England! Pilots make the best of a sunny July day at Ashford. (John Quincy)

Right: A four-gun anti-aircraft site at Ashford. The .50-calibre guns were mounted on a trailer, the combination being officially known as a Multiple Carriage M-51. (John Quincy)

Right: The 'line shuttle' that collected ground personnel from around the Ashford strip and conveyed them to and from the mess sites. The 6 x 6 truck on the macadamed section of the perimeter track carries a rather pathetic example of the yellow warning flags required on all vehicles moving on the landing ground. Some of the men carry rifles, indicative of official concern about possible enemy paratroop landings. (Stan Wyglendowski)

Left: Armed group officers enjoying refreshment near the briefing area at Ashford. The nose of the CO's Thunderbolt, *Skirty Birt*, can be seen in the background. (Stan Wyglendowski)

Right: Ammunition and light ordnance storage beneath camouflage netting beside the Ashford strip, May 1944. (Stan Wyglendowski)

406th FIGHTER GROUP

Right, upper: P-47s of the 406th FG arrive over the Tour-en-Bessin strip, July 1944. (John Quincy)

Right, lower: First stop between distinctively manicured French elms, not far from Omaha beach. (John Quincy)

Above: A convoy bound for Normandy leaves the Solent: a view from the *Lucius Q. C. Lamar*, a US military transport which carried the 406th FG's personnel. (John Quincy)

Right: Lieutenant John Quincy, the 514th FS Supply Officer, had a fully loaded Jeep in the convoy of vehicles awaiting the order to move for loading at the port of embarkation, Southampton, in July 1944. (John Quincy)

Left: The GI washing line in a French orchard at A-13 Tour-en-Bessin. (John Quincy)

Right: French people from the surrounding neighbourhood spend a bright Sunday afternoon in early September watching mechanics inspect and service a newly delivered Thunderbolt at A-36 St Léonard. P-47D 44-19733 went missing in action on 27 December 1944. (John Quincy)

Left: An appropriate sign outside the 514th FS HQ tent at A-36 St Léonard. Apparently the Intelligence Section did not know the official names of some of the group's locations. Coigny was a village south of A-14 Cretteville, and Louplande was close to the domestic sites at A-36. (John Quincy)

Left: A café near Louplande, possibly at Le Fletch or Le Mans, put up this welcome for customers from the nearby airstrip. (John Quincy)

Above: There were always willing hands to take in GI laundry to earn a few dollars. Here a French-woman is paid for her labours when the laundry cart returns to Mourmelon-le-Grand on a freezing January day in 1945. (John Quincy)

Right: Coal slag heaps dot the horizon at bleak Asch, Belgium, where the 406th spent the early months of 1945. Here there was time to add colourful markings to the aircraft. The flamboyant *Big Ass Bird* of the 513th FS has the squadron's red nose swept back.

The red, blue and yellow horizontal bars on the vertical tail were adopted as a group marking. (John Quincy)

Above: Yellow-nose P-47D 42-28887 of the 512th FS at Asch. (John Quincy)

Right: The 514th FS dispersal area at Asch, with the re-arming of Thunderbolts in progress. The nearest P-47D is 44-20428. (John Quincy)

Above: *Little Ann* of 512th FS being serviced by its ground crew. The C-47B in the background, 43-16364, was in use by the HQ staff of the US 1st Army for liaison purposes when photographed at Asch; this aircraft was still flying a half century later. (John Quincy)

Above: *Angie*, a colourful Thunderbolt of the 512th FS, at rest at Asch. (John Quincy)

Below: A former gun emplacement on the outskirts of Brussels is used as a notice board for communist anti-monarchy slogans as well as a hoarding with a cautionary message for Allied troops. (John Quincy)

Above: At Asch timber and plywood prefabricated buildings from the US were erected as barracks—a welcome improvement on tents in a European winter.

The roofing sections were covered with bituminous felt. (John Quincy)

Below: The revised 514th FS squadron sign acknowledging the German location. The two officers are Captains White (right) and Smith. (John Quincy)

Left: Engine checks on P-47D 42-28401 '07-B' at Handorf, Germany, April 1945. (John Quincy)

Right: Notices such as this were intended to capitalize on the irony of the situation: Münster, about 15 April 1945. (John Quincy)

Left: Luftwaffe hangars offered the best maintenance cover the 406th ever had. Even so, some repair tasks were still carried out in the open. Here a Cletrac is ready with its hoist for an engine change. (John Quincy)

Above: A novel form of white surrender flag in the Adolf Hitler Strasse, Münster, April 1945. (John Quincy)

Above: Captain Bloom in his *Bloom's Tomb* at Handorf in April 1945. (John Quincy)

bolts are here seen parked around the concrete and tarmac apron. (John Quincy)

Right: The 406th FG's final move was to Nordholz, where 514th FS Thunder-

All John Quincy photographs in this section via Stan Wyglendowski

Left: Colonel C. B. Kelly, 406th FG CO, in his personal P-47D, *Skirty Birt*, at Handorf. (John Quincy)

Right: Lieutenant Quincy waiting on the flight line at Nordholz for aircraft to return. The Cessna UC-78 in the background, 43-32083, was assigned to the group for communications work. (John Quincy)

409th
BOMBARDMENT GROUP

640th, 641st, 642nd and 643rd Bombardment Squadrons

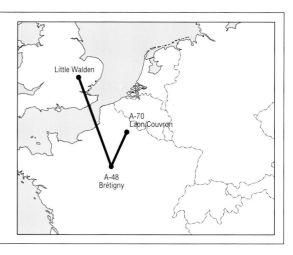

Left to right: 640th, 641st and 643rd Bombardment Squadron insignia.

410th
BOMBARDMENT GROUP

644th, 645th, 646th and 647th Bombardment Squadrons

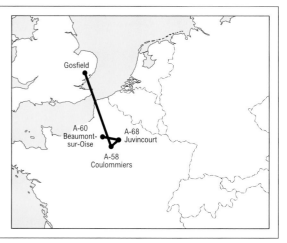

Left to right: Insignia of the 644th, 645th and 646th Bombardment Squadrons.

Right: Insignia of the 647th BS.

Far right: An A-20G Havoc of the 647th BS on its Gosfield hardstand. (410th BG Association)

416th
BOMBARDMENT GROUP

668th, 669th, 670th and 671st Bombardment Squadrons

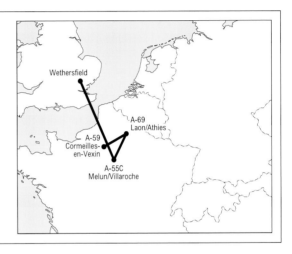

Below: A black rudder distinguished the Douglas Invaders of the 416th BG. A-26B *For Pete's Sake!* was photographed at Chalgrove, England in the spring of 1945. (Robert Astrella)

434th
TROOP CARRIER GROUP

71st, 77nd, 73rd and 74th Troop Carrier Squadrons

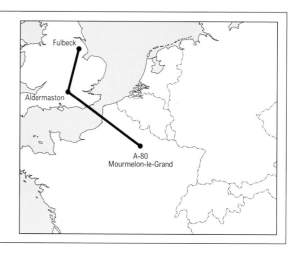

Below: A C-47A of the 74th TCS on a visit to Mount Farm, England. The underwing racks used for carrying parapacks (equipment containers dropped by parachute) are clearly visible in this photograph. (Robert Astrella)

435th
TROOP CARRIER GROUP

75th, 76th, 77th and 78th Troop Carrier Squadrons

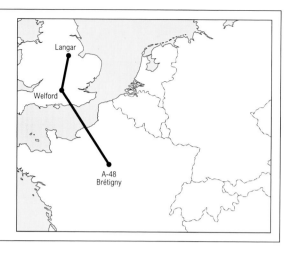

Left to right: 75th, 76th and 77th Troop Carrier Squadron insignia.

436th
TROOP CARRIER GROUP

79th, 80th, 81st and 82nd Troop Carrier Squadrons

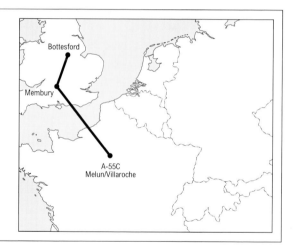

Right: The unofficial insignia of the 436th TCG painted on the end wall of a building in the technical site at Welford. (Dave Benfield)

Far right: C-47s of the 81st and 82nd TCSs on a Continental airfield. (James Bingman)

437th
TROOP CARRIER GROUP

83rd, 84th, 85th and 86th Troop Carrier Squadrons

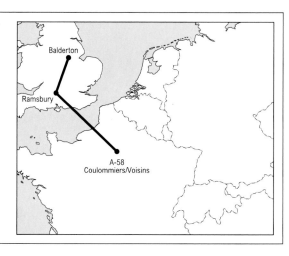

Above: C-47 pilots Lieutenant Don Handigard and Lieutenant 'Cozy' Cole of the 437th TCG outside a Nissen hut on a domestic site at Ramsbury, spring 1944. Handigard was killed when shot down during the D-Day airborne operations in the only 437th aircraft lost. The Nissen hut ends are boarded and covered with bituminous felt. Among the crew bicycles, a common sight around aircrew barracks in England at the time, is one up-ended for tyre repairs—another familiar sight, owing to the poor quality of wartime British cycle tyres. (Richard Denison)

Right: C-47A 42-100806 '90-M' at Nordholz, Germany, in May 1945. After the war this aircraft was used by the Peruvian Air Force for many years. (John Quincy)

Right: Captain Joe Antrim, Operations Officer of the 85th TCS, took this photograph of his D-Day crew shortly after the event. Standing in front of C-47 42-100806 are, left to right, Lieutenant Floyd Kelly, pilot; Lieutenant 'Steve' Stevens, co-pilot; and Lieutenant Joe Salisbury, the navigator. Kneeling are Sergeant Don Bolce, the radio operator; and Sergeant George Montgomery, the crew chief. (Joseph C. Antrim via the Wilts and Berks Research Group)

438th
TROOP CARRIER GROUP

87th, 88th, 89th and 90th Troop Carrier Squadrons

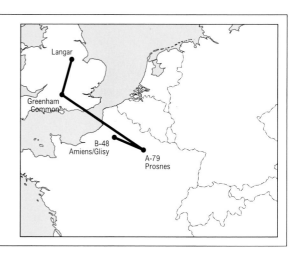

Above: *Sugar Puss* and her crew at Greenham Common. This aircraft, leaving the United States in 1943 to fly the North Atlantic via Iceland and the United Kingdom, went on to Tunisia as a replacement aircraft in the 18th TCS of the 64th TCG. In April 1944 it was transferred to the 90th TCS at Greenham Common. Lieutenant Gilbert Estelle, the pilot, and S/Sergeant Gordon Jordan, the radio operator, were members of the original crew that had been assigned to the aircraft in July 1943, when Estelle was the co-pilot. *Sugar Puss* towed a Horsa to Normandy on 7 June 1944 and sustained some flak damage. It took part in all the major airborne operations in the ETO and had over 1,000 hours' flying time. After the war the aircraft was used as a civilian freighter and was destroyed in a crash on 8 March 1948 when it hit a mountain at San Jose, California. In the photograph Gilbert Estelle is the officer in the centre of the group. (Gilbert Estelle)

439th
TROOP CARRIER GROUP

91st, 92nd, 93rd and 94th Troop Carrier Squadrons

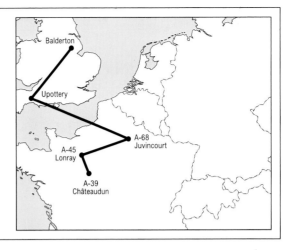

Above: Two C-47s of the 93rd TCS flying over Essex in the spring of 1944. (Ed Ritchie)

440th

TROOP CARRIER GROUP

95th, 96th, 97th and 98th Troop Carrier Squadrons

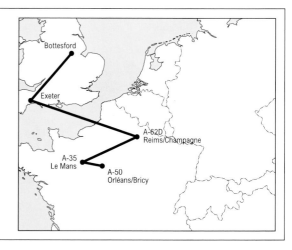

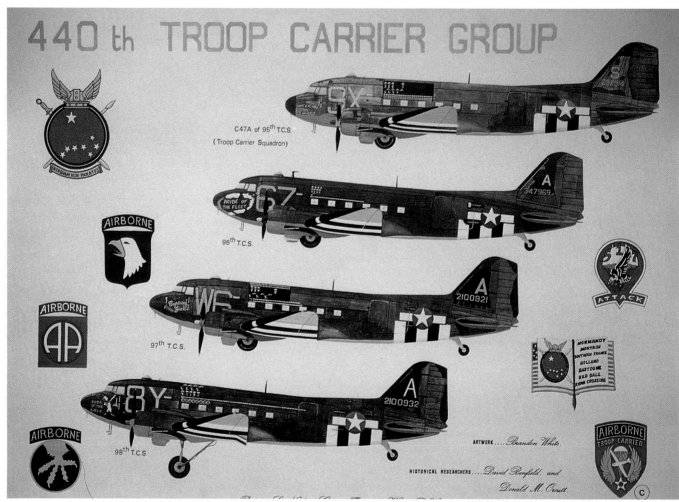

Above: A post-war poster featuring a C-47 from each of the 440th TCG's four squadrons that operated from Exeter. (Brandon White)

441st
TROOP CARRIER GROUP
99th, 100th, 301st and 302nd Troop Carrier Squadrons

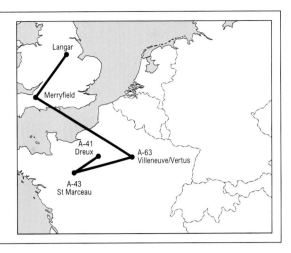

Left: C-47s of the 99th TCS in flight over Italy when the unit was temporarily transferred to the Mediterranean theatre in preparation for the airborne landings in southern France. The photograph was taken when personnel of a fighter group were being transferred to another base. (Ira LaTour)

442nd
TROOP CARRIER GROUP
303rd, 304th, 305th and 306th Troop Carrier Squadrons

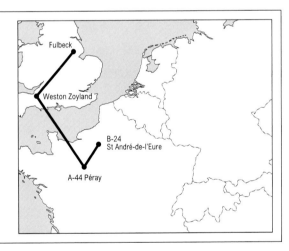

Left: C-47A 42-92879, resplendent in full D-Day stripes, visiting Mount Farm, England, in the summer of 1944. This was an aircraft of the 303rd TCS which was scrapped in June 1946. (Robert Astrella)

Above: Waco CG-4A gliders marshalled on Chilbolton airfield in early September 1944, ready for the 442nd TCG to use in Operation 'Market'. This photograph was taken from a B-26 taking off on runway 12 to the north-west. Many of these gliders have had the Allied Expeditionary Air Force's stripes above the wings painted out, indicating that the aircraft had previously been prepared for the 6 June invasion. (George Kammermeyer)

Below: Chilbolton airfield loaded with Waco CG-4A gliders for the 442nd to use in Operation 'Market': a view looking west. (George Kammermeyer)

474th
FIGHTER GROUP

428th, 429th and 430th Fighter Squadrons

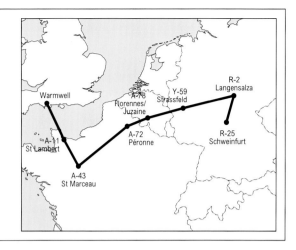

Left to right: Insignia of the 428th, 429th and 430th Fighter Squadrons. The P-38 cartoons in these emblems have the colours which identified each squadron's aircraft.

422nd
NIGHT FIGHTER SQUADRON

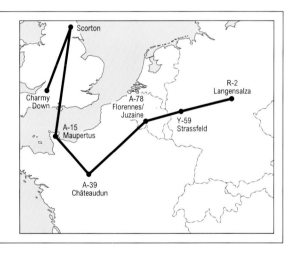

Right: One of the original P-61A Black Widows received by the 422nd NFS taxies past Podington control tower, England, July 1944. This aircraft, 42-5558, is painted in the early olive drab and neutral grey finish with an opaque nose cover over the radar scanner. (William Furness)

Right: The 422nd NFS was the first to be equipped with the P-61A in Europe and 42-5565, nicknamed *Double Trouble*, was an early assignment. The crew chief was Sergeant E. W. McLain and the aircraft was usually flown by 1/Lt Robert G. Bolinder. It was photographed by Charles E. Brown for the British magazine *Aeronautics* early in September 1944 while flying over the coast east of the squadron's base, Maupertus, on the Cotentin Peninsula. Bolinder later achieved credits for the destruction of four enemy aircraft, two during the night of 17 December 1944. (C. E. Brown)

Below: To supplement its P-61 Black Widows—which were in short supply during the winter of 1944–45— the 422nd NFS received a small number of A-20G Havocs. These were used principally for intruder operations and occasionally for dropping flares to aid US Army artillery. This one, photographed during a visit to Debden, England, wore a glossy black finish which was deemed to be the most effective disguise if the aircraft were caught in searchlights. (Ed Ritchie)

425th
NIGHT FIGHTER SQUADRON

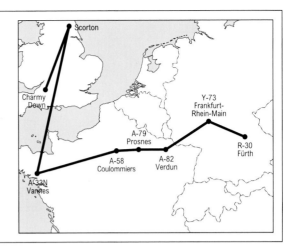

Left: P-61A 42-5570 on one of the concrete dispersals at A-33N Vannes, France, that had served the Luftwaffe only a few weeks before this photograph was taken. (USAF)

Right: P-61B *Hel'N Back* at Fürth, Germany in the spring of 1945, bearing seven mission symbols for intruder attacks during the last weeks of the war. It is equipped with P-38 drop tanks to give a better endurance. (Link Derick)

Above: Armourers loading a magazine with 20mm cannon shell for P-61A *Dangerous Dan*. The four cannon were supplied with 20 rounds per gun. Originally the P-61 also had four .50-calibre guns in a barbette behind the flight deck, but these were removed because of buffeting problems when the guns were traversed; the weapons also tended to 'blind' the pilot temporarily by their glare when they were fired. (USAF)

Right: Resplendent in its glossy black finish, *Tabitha* rests at Vannes in October 1944. This P-61 had but a brief operational career, being written off in an accident before the end of the year.

INDEXES

INDEX OF PERSONS

Storrie, Carl R., (323/387BG),
31
Swenson, Lt, (397BG), 119

Tipton, James B., (358FG), 64

Vasumpaur, George, (387BG),
108

Wagner, Walter, 123
Waller, Cpl, (358FG), 64
White, Capt., (406FG), 137
Witherbee, Dale B., (344BG),
53
Willard, Chaplain, (316TCG),
26
Wojack, Sgt, (344BG), 47

Wood, A. J., (323BG), 53
Woodrum, W. J., (323BG), 38
Woolner, Ralph ('Jack'),
(10PG), 14
Wright, Harold H., (314TCG),
23

Young, W., (344BG), 50

INDEX OF PLACENAMES

Ahrweiler (Germany), 110
Andrews Field, 28
Asch (Belgium), 70, 72, 132,
134, 136, 137
Ashford, 125, 126

Beaulieu, 33
Beaumont-sur-Oise (France),
95, 96, 97
Boxted, 60, 61
Brest (France), 66
Brussels (Belgium), 136

Chalgrove, 14, 143
Charleroi (France), 49
Chelmsford, 117
Chièvres (Belgium), 71, 114
Chilbolton, 152
Chipping Ongar, 31, 105, 106,
109
Clastres (France), 76, 77, 79
Coigny (France), 131
Cologne (Germany), 33
Corcelles-Seine (France), 43
Cormeilles-en-Vexin (France),
45, 47, 51
Cottesmore, 27

Cretteville (France), 131

Dayton (USA), 115

Earls Colne, 30, 31

Forêt de Grimbosq (France),
107
Fürth (Germany), 12, 80, 87

Genicourt (France), 45
Gosfield, 143
Great Dunmow, 90, 92
Greenham Common, 148

Handorf (Germany), 139, 141
Hanover (Germany), 88
Headcorn, 65, 69
Heuringham (France), 57

Juvincourt (France), 74

Laon (France), 33, 34, 37
Le Fletch France), 132
Le Mans (France), 132
Lippstadt (Germany), 88
Louplande (France), 131, 132

Magdeburg (Germany), 119
Mannheim/Sandorf (Germany),
63
Maupertus (France),154
Mourmelon-le -Grand (France),
79, 132
Mount Farm, 15, 144
Münster (Germany), 73, 139

Nancy (France), 17
Nordholz (Germany), 21, 111,
113
Nuremberg (Germany), 64

Oakham, 26
Old Buckenham, 27

Péronne (France), 9, 116,
119, 120
Prosnes (France), 66
Podington, 61, 75
Poix (France), 24

Ramsbury, 146

St Dizier (France), 10, 14, 83,
124

St Léonard (France), 130, 131
St Mawgan, 59
Ste Mère-Église (France), 78
St Omer (France), 57
St Trond (Belgium), 99, 100,
103, 123
St Wendle (France), 92
Sandhofen (Germany), 64
Shaftesbury, 111
Southampton, 128
Spanhoe, 256
Stansted, 38, 43, 46, 48, 49,
50, 51, 53, 54, 55
Steeple Morden, 46, 120
Stoney Cross, 108
Straubing (Germany), 69, 84

Toul/Ochey (France), 17, 18,
19
Tour-en-Bessin (France), 128,
130

Welford, 145
Weymouth, 43
Wormingford, 65, 66

INDEX OF AIRCRAFT NAMES
*Model, tail number, codes, squadron and group are given in
parentheses, where known and applicable*

Angie (P-47D 226860 'L3-
0',315FS/406FG), 136
'Azel (F-6C,2103213, 'IX-
H',162TRS/10PRG), 12

Bat-outa-hell II (B-26B 131643
'YU-G', 455BS/323BG), 31
Betty (P-47, 379FS/362FG),
66
Big Ass Bird (P-47D 432773

'4P-S', 513FS/406FG), 132
Big Hairy Bird, The, (B-26B
296165 '6B-T', 599BS/
397BG), 109, 120
Bingo Buster (B-26C 134863
'RJ-P', 454BS/323BG), 30
Bloom's Tomb (P-47B 228401
'07-B', 514FS/406FG), 140
Bonnie B (P-51B 312457 'FT-
E', 353FS/354FG), 61

Bucephalus II (P-47D, 379FS/
362FG), 67
Bunny's Honey (B-26B 295875
'Y5-Q', 495BS/344BG), 53
Buzzard, The, (B-26B 295909
'Y5-G', 495BS/344BG), 48

Clark's Little Pill (B-26C
134959 'SS-Q', 451BS/
322BG), 28

Crew 13 (B-26B 131969 'WT-
S', 456BS/323BG), 35

Dangerous Dan (P-61A,
425NFS), 155
Danny Boy (P-47D, 379FS/
362FG), 69
Deacon, The, (P-47D, 379FS/
362FG), 67
Dee Feater (B-26B 296142